Simple Reflections

A Journal for Memories and Musings

KIM DIEHL

Mini Breakfast Quiches

These little quiches have become a favorite with my family, and I especially love the convenience of freezing and reheating them in the microwave for grab-and-go breakfasts. For a fantastic option for holiday brunch, prepare the muffin tins and filling the night before, keeping them separate, and then refrigerate. Fill the crusts in the morning and bake. Easy!

3 refrigerated ready-to-bake
   rolled piecrusts
10 large eggs
½ cup milk (fat-free half-and-
   half also works well)
1 teaspoon salt
½ teaspoon pepper
1 12-ounce package frozen
   chopped spinach, thawed
1 cup diced cooked ham
½ cup cooked and crumbled
   bacon
1 small zucchini, shredded
½ cup red bell pepper,
   finely diced
2 green onions, cut lengthwise and sliced (including greens)
2 cups shredded cheddar cheese
½ cup (approximately) shredded Parmesan cheese for topping

Preheat oven to 400°. Lightly spray two 12-cup muffin tins with nonstick cooking spray. Use a 4" biscuit cutter to cut rounds from the crusts, rerolling and using the scraps to make 24. Gently push a crust round into each muffin cavity. In a large bowl, beat the eggs, milk, salt, and pepper. Use layers of paper towel to squeeze the liquid from the spinach. Stir the spinach and all remaining ingredients except the Parmesan cheese into the eggs. Use an ice cream scoop to evenly portion the egg mixture into the prepared muffin cups. Add a pinch of Parmesan cheese onto each quiche. Bake 25 minutes, until golden brown. Makes 24 quiches.

Chocolate Chip Snowball Cookies

Years ago when I was craving a big, soft chocolate chip cookie, I created this recipe, and then spent years tweaking the ingredients to get it just right. While these are great straight out of the oven, they become very soft and almost cake like when stored in an airtight container for a day . . . that is, if you can find the willpower to wait!

2 cups granulated sugar
1 cup (2 sticks) butter, softened
8 ounces Neufchatel cheese
    or cream cheese
¼ cup sour cream (I use light)
4 eggs
2 teaspoons vanilla
½ teaspoon almond extract
7 cups flour
4 teaspoons baking powder
1 teaspoon baking soda
1 teaspoon salt
1 bag (11.5 ounces) milk-chocolate chips
    (or even more, if you'd like to be decadent)
⅓ cup additional granulated sugar for rolling

Preheat oven to 375°F. In a large mixer bowl, beat 2 cups sugar, butter, Neufchatel cheese, and sour cream on medium speed until fluffy. Beat in eggs, one at a time, until combined. Stir in vanilla and almond extract. In a separate bowl, combine flour, baking powder, baking soda, and salt; add to wet mixture in three additions, beating well after each addition. Stir in chocolate chips. Cover dough with plastic wrap and refrigerate one hour. Roll dough into ping-pong-ball sized balls, and then roll in granulated sugar to coat; place 2" apart on ungreased cookie sheets. Bake for approximately 10 minutes, or just until set and very lightly browned on the bottom—don't overbake! Makes about 5 dozen soft and yummy cookies, depending upon the size you roll them.

My Best Apple Pie

When cool weather arrives, my husband's very favorite pie is Dutch apple—so I spent years experimenting and tweaking my recipe until he let me know one day that it was the best apple pie he'd ever had. Success!

PIE

1½ cups water
¼ cup cornstarch
½ cup sugar
1 rounded teaspoon ground
    cinnamon
¼ teaspoon salt
2 teaspoons lemon juice
8 cups peeled and thickly
    sliced (about ¼")
    Granny Smith apples
4 tablespoons salted butter,
    cut into small pieces
1 purchased 9" refrigerated
    piecrust

TOPPING

½ cup (1 stick) cold salted butter
¾ cup flour
½ cup quick-cooking rolled oats
½ cup brown sugar, packed

Preheat oven to 350°. Mix water, cornstarch, sugar, cinnamon, salt, and lemon juice in a large saucepan. Bring to a boil over medium-high heat, whisking constantly; cook 1 minute, until thickened. Add apples. Cover and cook 5 minutes, stirring often so bottom apples don't scorch. Add diced butter and stir until melted into filling mixture. Pour filling into a pie plate lined with crust. Cut cold butter into the remaining topping ingredients until well blended and crumbly; sprinkle over apple filling. If desired, use a cookie cutter to cut shapes from an extra piecrust to "pretty up" your pie. Bake on a foil-lined cookie sheet 50 to 60 minutes, until golden brown and bubbly, covering crust edges during a portion of the baking time if needed to prevent them from overbrowning. Serve with a scoop of vanilla ice cream.

Raspberry Kiss Thumbprint Cookies

Years ago during a holiday baking binge, I went on a quest for the perfect thumbprint cookie. When I couldn't find exactly what I was envisioning, I adapted my Chocolate Chip Snowball Cookie recipe (page 16) and created my own version of this classic treat. The addition of the raspberry jam takes these completely over the top.

1 cup granulated sugar
½ cup (1 stick) butter, softened
4 ounces Neufchatel cheese or
    cream cheese
¼ cup sour cream (I use light)
2 eggs
1 teaspoon vanilla
1/4 teaspoon almond extract
3½ cups plus 1 tablespoon flour
2 teaspoons baking powder
½ teaspoon baking soda
½ teaspoon salt
¼ cup seedless raspberry jam
1 bag (12 ounces) Hershey's Kisses
¼ cup additional granulated sugar for rolling

Remove wrappers from chocolate pieces. Preheat oven to 375°F. In a large mixer bowl, beat 1 cup sugar, butter, Neufchatel cheese, and sour cream on medium speed until fluffy. Beat in eggs, one at a time, until combined. Stir in vanilla and almond extract. In a separate bowl, combine the flour, baking powder, baking soda, and salt; add to wet mixture in two or three additions, beating well after each addition. Cover dough with plastic wrap and refrigerate one hour. Roll dough into walnut-sized balls, and then roll in granulated sugar to coat. Use your thumb or the back of a spoon to make a slight indentation in the top of each ball, and then fill with approximately ¼ teaspoon of raspberry jam. Bake on ungreased cookie sheets for approximately 10 minutes or just until set and very lightly browned on the bottom. While cookies are still warm, lightly press a Hershey's Kiss into center of each one. Makes approximately 3 dozen cookies.

Homemade Mocha Mix

Real bits of shaved chocolate add a rich, decadent flavor to this yummy cool-weather treat. For gifting, spoon the mix into a jar, add a small cellophane bag of mini marshmallows, and include peppermint sticks for stirring. Be sure to add a small tag with instructions to combine ⅓ cup of mix with 1 cup of boiling water.

1½ rounded cups cocoa powder (I like Dutch processed)
2 rounded cups powdered sugar
⅔ cup instant coffee
1 rounded cup powdered milk
⅔ cup dark or semisweet chocolate pieces, shaved from a bar
¾ teaspoon salt

Gently mix ingredients in a medium bowl (to avoid coating your kitchen with powdered sugar!) and store in an airtight jar or container. Prepare your mocha as noted above, stirring until the chocolate melts, and then savor each sip.

Buttery Caramel Corn

When autumn rolls around, so does my craving for this crunchy, buttery treat. Be warned, once you start munching on these little nuggets of goodness, it's hard to stop!

2 bags, 3.5 ounces each, microwave popcorn, popped
(Blast O Butter is completely fabulous for this recipe)
2 sticks salted butter (not margarine!)
2 cups packed brown sugar
½ cup light corn syrup
Pinch of cream of tartar

Preheat the oven to 200°. Spray a large roasting pan with nonstick cooking spray. Pour popcorn into the prepared roaster, picking out any visible unpopped kernels; set aside. In a saucepan, melt butter, brown sugar, and corn syrup. Bring to a boil and simmer over medium heat 5 minutes, stirring occasionally. Remove from heat and stir in cream of tartar. Pour mixture over popcorn. Stir gently but well. Bake uncovered 1 hour, stirring every 15 minutes. Pour into a large serving bowl. This also makes great Halloween treats for the kiddos in your life when poured into little cellophane bags and tied up with a bow.

Sugared Pecans

One of my hands-down favorite holiday treats is sugared pecans, and I'm happy to share my easy recipe for these yummy morsels. Warning: These are highly habit-forming, but if you're able to part with some of them, they make great gifts when wrapped in cellophane bags and tied up with pretty little bows.

2 egg whites
1 tablespoon water
1 pound pecan halves
1 cup granulated white sugar
1 teaspoon salt
¾ teaspoon ground cinnamon

Preheat oven to 250°F. Lightly grease or coat a baking sheet with nonstick cooking spray. In a gallon-sized plastic zipper bag, mix sugar, salt, and cinnamon. In a large bowl with the mixer set on high, whip egg whites and water until frothy. (This only takes about a minute!) Add pecans to whipped egg whites and stir until coated. Pour pecans into the bag of sugar mixture and toss until coated. Spread coated pecans on the prepared baking sheet and bake at 250° for 1 hour, stirring every 15 minutes. Serve in a bowl, or ladle cooled pecans into cellophane gift bags and tie with ribbons.

Gingerbread Cake with Vanilla Sauce

To me, nothing says Christmas quite like gingerbread. I've been baking this holiday treat for years, and the vanilla sauce is the icing on the cake . . . literally! For another great option, divide the batter between two or three mini loaf pans, and then drop the cooled loaves into cellophane bags for gifts.

CAKE
1 cup sour cream (I use light)
½ cup packed brown sugar
1 egg
½ cup molasses
1½ cups flour
1 teaspoon each cinnamon,
    ginger, salt, and baking soda

VANILLA SAUCE
½ cup (1 stick) butter
½ cup granulated sugar
½ cup packed brown sugar
½ cup heavy cream
⅛ teaspoon salt
Pinch of nutmeg (if desired)
2 teaspoons vanilla

Preheat oven to 350°F. In a medium bowl, use a mixer on medium speed to blend the first four cake ingredients. Add remaining cake ingredients and mix until blended. Pour batter into a greased and floured 9" pan, either square or round, and bake 30 to 40 minutes or until cake tests done with a toothpick. While cake is baking, combine all sauce ingredients except vanilla in a small saucepan. Cook over medium heat, stirring occasionally, until the mixture comes to a boil; then remove from heat and add vanilla. The sauce will thicken as it cools. To serve, drizzle warm sauce over individual pieces of cake. Refrigerate any leftover sauce.

Christmas Cashew Toffee

When the holidays roll around, this treat is the first thing my family asks for. When you begin munching on these little nuggets of crunchy goodness, it's almost impossible to stop, so my best advice is to give in and enjoy it! And then break out your stretchy pants.

1 pound (4 sticks) salted butter (no substitute)
1½ cups granulated sugar
2 tablespoons water
1 cup lightly salted cashews, rough chopped
1 cup milk-chocolate chips
½ cup salted cashews, finely chopped, for topping

Combine the first three ingredients in a large nonstick skillet and cook over medium-high heat until a candy thermometer registers 315°F, stirring occasionally (this takes about 7 to 10 minutes). If you don't have a candy thermometer, the toffee should be done when it's the color of a brown paper bag. Turn off the heat and quickly stir in the chopped cashews; pour into a flexible, metal, nonstick 9"×13" baking sheet with a rim. Let rest 2 or 3 minutes before sprinkling with milk-chocolate chips. After the chips are all melty, spread them over the toffee. Sprinkle with the finely chopped cashews. Refrigerate until cool and the chocolate is set, usually 2 to 3 hours. Flex the pan to pop the toffee out and break it into pieces.

Baked Donuts with Chocolate Icing

Fall is my favorite season for baking, especially on crisp, cool mornings. What better way to wake your family than with the smell of freshly brewed coffee and yummy donuts baking in the oven?

DONUTS
1⅓ cups flour
½ rounded cup granulated sugar
½ teaspoon baking soda
½ teaspoon baking powder
½ teaspoon salt
1 teaspoon vanilla
1 egg
⅓ cup sour cream (I use light)
¼ cup plus 1 teaspoon milk
¼ cup vegetable oil

CHOCOLATE ICING
1¾ cups powdered sugar
3 tablespoons milk (I use fat-free half-and-half)
2 rounded tablespoons of unsweetened cocoa
¼ teaspoon vanilla
½ teaspoon instant decaf coffee, dissolved in 1 tablespoon
    hot water
¼ teaspoon salt

Preheat oven to 375°. Spray 2 donut pans (six cavities each) with nonstick cooking spray. Combine the flour, sugar, baking soda, baking powder, and salt in a large mixing bowl. In a small mixing bowl, stir together the remaining ingredients until blended. Pour wet mix into dry mix and stir just until blended. Spoon the batter into a quart-size zippered plastic storage bag and seal. Snip the bag corner and pipe batter into the donut cavities until barely level with the center. Bake 8 to 9 minutes, until donuts are just set and springy. Cool donuts in pans 5 minutes; transfer to a wax paper–lined rack to cool. Whisk icing ingredients together in a small bowl. Working quickly, use a butter knife to spread icing onto the top half of each donut before frosting sets. Makes approximately 9 or 10 donuts. Enjoy!

Pumpkin Cream Cheese Muffins

*I love all things pumpkin, and these moist and tasty muffins are
no exception. A dollop of cream cheese filling and a sprinkling
of chocolate chips make them irresistible.*

MUFFINS
2 cups flour
1 rounded tablespoon pumpkin pie spice
1 teaspoon salt
1 teaspoon baking soda
1 15-ounce can pumpkin puree
¾ cup packed brown sugar
¾ cup granulated sugar
2 large eggs, plus the white of one
    additional egg (reserve the yolk)
½ cup vegetable oil
2 teaspoons vanilla extract

FILLING
8 ounces cream cheese, softened
⅓ cup granulated sugar
1 egg yolk (reserved from above)
1 teaspoon vanilla extract

TOPPING
½ cup semisweet chocolate chips or mini chips

Preheat oven to 375°. Line 20 muffin cups with paper liners.
In a medium bowl, whisk together flour, pumpkin pie spice,
salt, and baking soda. In a large bowl, whisk together pumpkin,
granulated sugar, and brown sugar. Add the remaining muffin
ingredients to the large bowl and stir until blended. Stir the dry
mix into the wet mix until just blended. In a medium bowl,
blend all filling ingredients until smooth. Fill lined muffin cups
two-thirds full with batter. Combine the filling ingredients. Add
a dollop of filling (approximately 1 tablespoon) to the top of
each muffin and swirl it with a toothpick. Add a small sprinkle
of chocolate chips to the centers of the muffins. Bake 18 to 20
minutes, until nicely rounded and muffins test done with a
toothpick. Cool in pans until room temperature, and then
transfer pans to the refrigerator to set the chocolate chips. Store
covered in the refrigerator. Makes approximately 20 muffins.

Soft and Chewy Peanut Butter Cookies

There's something about peanut butter cookies that just screams fall to me, and these soft and chewy cookies are the best I've ever had. This recipe makes quite a few cookies, but they're so yummy they'll be gone before you can say "pass the stretchy pants."

1 cup (2 sticks) salted butter, softened
1¾ cups creamy peanut butter
2 eggs
1½ cups packed brown sugar
1 cup granulated sugar
3¼ cups flour
1 tablespoon baking powder
1 teaspoon salt
Additional sugar for rolling cookies

Preheat oven to 350°. In a large bowl, mix the butter, peanut butter, eggs, and sugars until blended. In a medium bowl, sift the flour, baking powder, and salt. Add the dry ingredients to the wet mixture in three additions, just until blended. Roll dough into ping-pong-ball sized balls (about 1 rounded tablespoon). Pour additional sugar into a small mixing bowl. Roll cookies in sugar and place on cookie sheets lined with a baking sheet or parchment paper. Use a fork to lightly press the top of each cookie vertically and horizontally. Bake 9 to 10 minutes, until just set. Remove to wire racks to cool. Makes about 5 to 6 dozen, depending upon the size of your cookies.